I0410994

Informing the legislative debate since 1914

# The 2014 Ebola Outbreak: International and U.S. Responses

Tiaji Salaam-Blyther
Specialist in Global Health

August 26, 2014

Congressional Research Service

7-5700

www.crs.gov

R43697

# Summary

Ebola virus disease (Ebola or EVD) is a severe, often fatal disease that was first detected near the Ebola River in the Democratic Republic of the Congo (DRC) in 1976. Originating in animals, EVD is spread to and among humans through contact with the blood, secretions, organs, or other bodily fluids of those infected. It is not transmitted through the air. On March 22, 2014, the World Health Organization (WHO) announced that 49 people had contracted EVD in Guinea, West Africa, and 29 of them had died. As of mid-August, the virus had quickly spread to Liberia, Sierra Leone, and Nigeria.

The Ebola virus that is circulating in West Africa is not new, but the current Ebola outbreak has infected and killed more people than all previous Ebola outbreaks combined. As of August 20, 2014, the WHO reported that 2,615 people had contracted the disease, of whom over 1,427 have died, slightly less than the combined cases (2,387) and deaths (1,590) from previous outbreaks.

Although there are no drugs proven to prevent or treat EBV, health experts know how to contain it. The disease is spreading, however, because the health systems in the affected countries are ill-equipped to undertake requisite containment and disease surveillance measures. Years of neglect and armed conflict have weakened infrastructures, including health systems, in the affected countries, most prominently in Sierra Leone and Liberia. WHO estimated that the outbreak had likely begun in December 2013, but was belatedly reported in March 2014 due to poor disease detection and surveillance capacity.

In July 2014, two U.S. citizen health workers contracted Ebola in Liberia and were first provided medication that had shown promise in animal studies but that had not yet been tested in humans. They were evacuated to the United States to receive additional care. Debate in the United States has ensued regarding entry and exit rights of people infected with communicable diseases; whether the international community (including the United States) had responded early and effectively enough to contain the virus; the appropriate use of experimental drugs that had not yet been tested for human safety and effectiveness, including how to choose recipients of scarce and sometimes costly drug supplies and how to arrange dispensing to allow analysis of safety and effectiveness; and feasible approaches to accelerating drug and vaccine development and the scale-up of manufacturing capacity for investigational products.

The apportionment of most U.S. global health aid is determined by language in appropriations legislation and their accompanying conference reports, which direct the majority of health aid at particular diseases, leaving proportionately fewer resources for broader health system strengthening activities. While deliberating the appropriate response to ongoing Ebola outbreak, as well as FY2015 appropriations, Congress is likely to discuss how to balance support for bolstering weak health systems while directly addressing the health effects of Ebola. The FY2015 budget includes a $45 million request from the Centers for Disease Control and Prevention (CDC) for the newly announced Global Health Security agenda and a $50 million funding proposal for pandemic preparedness efforts implemented by the U.S. Agency for International Development (USAID). The USAID FY2015 budget request is roughly 30% lower than the FY2014 appropriation. This report discusses these funding issues and examines other related concerns, including the impact Ebola is having on other health problems, such as maternal and child mortality, and the capacity of U.S. agencies to respond rapidly to unforeseen events, like the Ebola outbreak, in light of budgetary constraints and spending directives.

# Contents

# Figures

# Tables

## Contacts

# Background

Ebola virus disease (Ebola or EVD) is a severe, often fatal disease that was first detected near the Ebola River in the Democratic Republic of the Congo (DRC) in 1976.[1] Originating in animals, EVD is spread to humans and among humans through contact with the blood, secretions, organs, or other bodily fluids of those infected. It is not transmitted through the air. Individuals who are not symptomatic are not contagious.

On March 22, 2014, the World Health Organization (WHO) announced that 49 people had contracted EVD in Guinea, West Africa and 29 of them had died. WHO estimated that the outbreak—the first in West Africa—had likely begun in December 2013, but was belatedly detected due to weak disease surveillance and detection capacity. As of mid-August, the virus had spread to Sierra Leone, Liberia, and Nigeria, infecting more than 2,000 people and killing over half of them (**Figure 1**). WHO cautions, however, that evidence from the field indicate that "the numbers of reported cases and deaths vastly underestimate the magnitude of the outbreak."[2]

**Figure 1. Ebola Outbreaks: 1976-2014, as Reported on August 22, 2014**

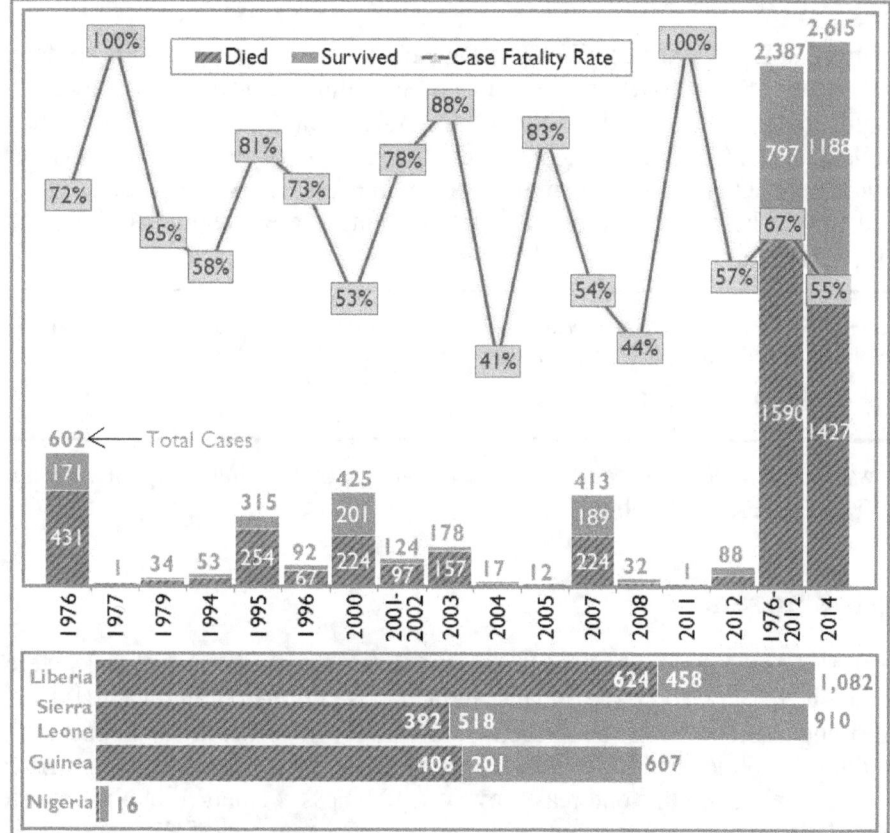

**Source:** Created by CRS from WHO, *Ebola Virus Disease*, fact sheet, number 103, April 2014 and WHO, *Ebola Virus Disease Update—West Africa*, August 22, 2014.

---

[1] This section was summarized from WHO, *Ebola*, fact sheet, number 103, April 2014.

[2] WHO, "No early end to the Ebola outbreak," Situation Assessment, August 14, 2014.

The rapid spread of this virus is of great concern to Congress. In August 2014, the House Foreign Affairs Subcommittee on Africa, Global Health, Global Human Rights, and International Organizations convened an emergency hearing on the subject. At the hearing, Members and witnesses discussed:

- the unprecedented scale of this outbreak;

- factors impeding country responses;

- whether the international community (including the United States) had responded early and effectively enough;

- the appropriate use of experimental drugs that had not yet been tested for human safety and effectiveness, including how to choose recipients of scarce drug supplies and how to arrange dispensing them safely and effectively; and

- prospects for developing cures and vaccines against the virus.[3]

The number of people who have contracted and succumbed to Ebola in this outbreak has exceeded the combined total of cases and deaths in all previous EVD outbreaks. New cases and deaths are reported regularly by WHO at http://www.who.int/csr/don/archive/disease/ebola/en/.

The Ebola virus that is circulating in West Africa is not new, and health experts are familiar with methods to contain it. Several factors make this outbreak unique, however, including (1) it is the first EVD outbreak to occur outside of East and Central Africa, (2) cases are spreading across borders simultaneously, (3) people are contracting the virus in urban areas, and (4) it has infected and killed more people than any other single EVD outbreak. The disease is spreading quickly, however, because the health systems in the affected countries are ill-equipped to implement requisite containment and disease surveillance measures.

> *"Standard measures, like early detection and isolation of cases, contact tracing and monitoring, and rigorous procedures for infection control, have stopped previous Ebola outbreaks and can do so again."*
>
> WHO Director-General, August 12, 2014

This report will discuss these issues and may be updated. For continuous updates on new EVD cases, see WHO site referenced above.

## Geographic Spread

Prior to the current outbreak in Guinea, Liberia, and Sierra Leone, EVD outbreaks were concentrated in the DRC, Gabon, the Sudans, and Uganda (**Figure 2**). In the current situation, Ebola is spreading in Sierra Leone and Liberia, particularly in border areas. In past outbreaks, people who discovered they had EVD after returning home from Central and East Africa did not spread the virus to others. In this outbreak, however, EVD cases emerged in Nigeria after a man infected with Ebola traveled to the country. No reports have emerged of EVD spreading in Saudi Arabia and Spain where EVD patients were evacuated after contracting the virus in Liberia.

---

[3] U.S. Congress, House Committee on Foreign Affairs, Subcommittee on Africa, Global Health, Global Human Rights and International Organizations, *Combating the Ebola Threat*, August 7, 2014.

## Border/Travel Issues

The shared borders of Guinea, Liberia, and Sierra Leone are notoriously porous and are the primary sites of Ebola transmission. Government officials in these countries have pledged to institute measures to prevent infected people from leaving their respective countries. WHO maintains that there is minimal risk of contracting Ebola on a plane,[4] though some countries are banning flights from the affected countries and are revoking visas of travelers from the area.[5] According to the State Department, fear about the virus is impacting peacekeeping and security efforts outside the affected region. The African Union, for example, reportedly cancelled a planned deployment of Sierra Leonean peacekeeping forces to Somalia amid fears of the virus.[6] Suspension of airline services and poor road conditions in the affected countries are also reportedly hindering some non-governmental organizations (NGOs) from moving staff and equipment within and between affected countries.

### Figure 2. Map of Current and Past Ebola Outbreaks

**Source:** Adapted by CRS from the Centers of Disease Control and Prevention (CDC) at http://www.cdc.gov/vhf/ebola/resources/distribution-map-guinea-outbreak.html.

The Centers for Disease Control and Prevention (CDC) has issued a Level 3 Travel Warning for Liberia, Guinea, and Sierra Leone, advising all Americans to avoid nonessential travel to those countries. It has issued a Level 2 Travel Warning for Nigeria, urging Americans to take enhanced precautions when traveling to the area.[7] Several foreign aid groups, including U.S.-based institutions, are evacuating personnel from the region. The U.S. Peace Corps began evacuating 340 volunteers stationed in Guinea, Liberia, and Sierra Leone in August 2014.[8] Also in August, the State Department issued a travel warning for Liberia, advising Americans to avoid non-essential travel to the country and began evacuating family members of U.S. Foreign Service personnel from the Liberia and Sierra Leone, though U.S. embassies remain open in all of the

---

[4] WHO, "WHO: Air travel is low-risk for Ebola transmission," Note for the Media, August 14, 2014 and WHO, "Statement on travel and transport in relation to Ebola virus disease (EVD) outbreak, August 18, 2014.

[5] "Ebola cited in suspension of 7,200 Haj visas for Africa," *Arab News*, August 6, 2014 and "WHO urges calm as Kenya bans contact with Ebola-affected countries," *The Guardian*, August 17, 2014.

[6] U.S. Congress, House Committee on Foreign Affairs, Subcommittee on Africa, Global Health, Global Human Rights and International Organizations, *Combating the Ebola Threat*, Testimony by Bisa Williams, Deputy Assistant Secretary, Bureau of African Affairs, Department of State, August 7, 2014.

[7] CDC updates its travel warnings as events warrant at http://wwwnc.cdc.gov/travel/diseases/ebola.

[8] Peace Corps, "Peace Corps Removing Volunteers in Liberia, Sierra Leone, and Guinea," press release, July 30, 2014.

affected countries.[9] Samaritan's Purse, a U.S. non-governmental organization (NGO), ended its healthcare efforts in Liberia after two of its staff contracted EVD while treating Ebola patients.

## Urban Spread

Previous human EVD outbreaks occurred in rural and forested areas. The current outbreak is spreading in rural and urban settings alike, including capitals. High density conditions in the capitals of Liberia and Sierra Leone are facilitating the rapid spread of the virus. Disease outbreaks in urban areas are also troublesome because of the role cities play in international travel, with many observers fearing importation of the virus via air travel.

# Health System Constraints in Affected Countries

A major factor in the rapid spread of Ebola among the affected countries is weak health system capacity. Guinea, Liberia, and Sierra Leone are among the poorest countries in the world. The infrastructure, including the health systems, of these countries has been decimated by years of conflict and neglect. Each of the countries had recently begun to enjoy modest fiscal growth and political stability. This section describes how deficits in each component of the affected countries' health systems enable the virus to continue to spread. **Table 1** summarizes these issues.[10]

**Table 1. Impact of Health System Deficiencies on Ebola Outbreak Containment**

| | Governance | Financing | Human Resources | Commodities | Service Delivery | Information |
|---|---|---|---|---|---|---|
| Description | Policies, strategies, and plans that inform the course of action a country will take to meet the health needs of its people. | Mechanisms used to fund health efforts and allocate resources. | The people who provide healthcare and support health delivery. | Goods that are used to provide healthcare. | The management and delivery of healthcare. | The collection, analysis, and dissemination of health statistics for planning and allocating health resources. |
| Impact of Health System Component Deficiency in Ebola Context | Slow initial government response to Ebola outbreak and insufficient capacity to implement national Ebola plans has further diminished public confidence in political authorities, limiting efforts to quell rumors and fears about Ebola and to carry out disease control. | Insufficient financial resources to fund local responses and pay health personnel contribute to human resource and commodity shortages. | Shortages of not only health personnel, but also support staff like grave diggers and statisticians limit the ability to detect, prevent, and treat EVD cases. | Insufficient supply of protective equipment threatens the safety of healthcare workers (including community volunteers) and is associated with hospital- and clinic-based infections. | Many health facilities in Liberia and Sierra Leone. In Monrovia, Liberia, all five major hospitals are closed and only three clinics were operating as of August 15. | Limited capacity to conduct contact tracing and diagnosis calls into question the actual EVD cases and impedes efforts to detect, treat, and control the virus. |

**Source:** Created by CRS from WHO webpage on health systems and research on the 2014 Ebola outbreak.

---

[9] State Department, "Response to the Ebola Virus," Fact Sheet, August 12, 2014. The State Department issues travel warnings and alerts as events warrant at http://travel.state.gov/content/passports/english/alertswarnings.html.

[10] For more information on health systems, see http://www.who.int/topics/health_systems/en/.

# Governance

Following civil unrest, public confidence in government institutions is typically low. Government leaders in Sierra Leone, Liberia, and Guinea are all working to restore public trust. Poor conditions in each of these countries, marked by limited and low-quality public services, frequent interruptions in water and electricity supply, impassable roads, and limited employment and investment opportunities, have further eroded faith in government. Considering low public trust of government institutions, public service messages and health outreach campaigns led by government officials have met resistance and skepticism, further undermining efforts to control the spread of Ebola. Reports of attacks on health workers and health facilities (run by aid workers and government officials alike) persist. Rather than reporting suspected Ebola cases to health officials, people have hidden the ill and patients have fled health facilities while undergoing treatment, fearing they would contract Ebola in the poorly-equipped health centers. Avoidance of health facilities is troubling to health experts not only for its impact on Ebola containment efforts, but also for the possible negative effects on other health efforts, including maternal and child health programs. Giving birth is particularly risky in the Ebola outbreak countries. Maternal mortality rates in these areas are among the highest in the world, with Sierra Leone having the highest (**Figure 3**).

**Figure 3. Health Statistics: Affected Countries, Africa, High-Income Countries, World**

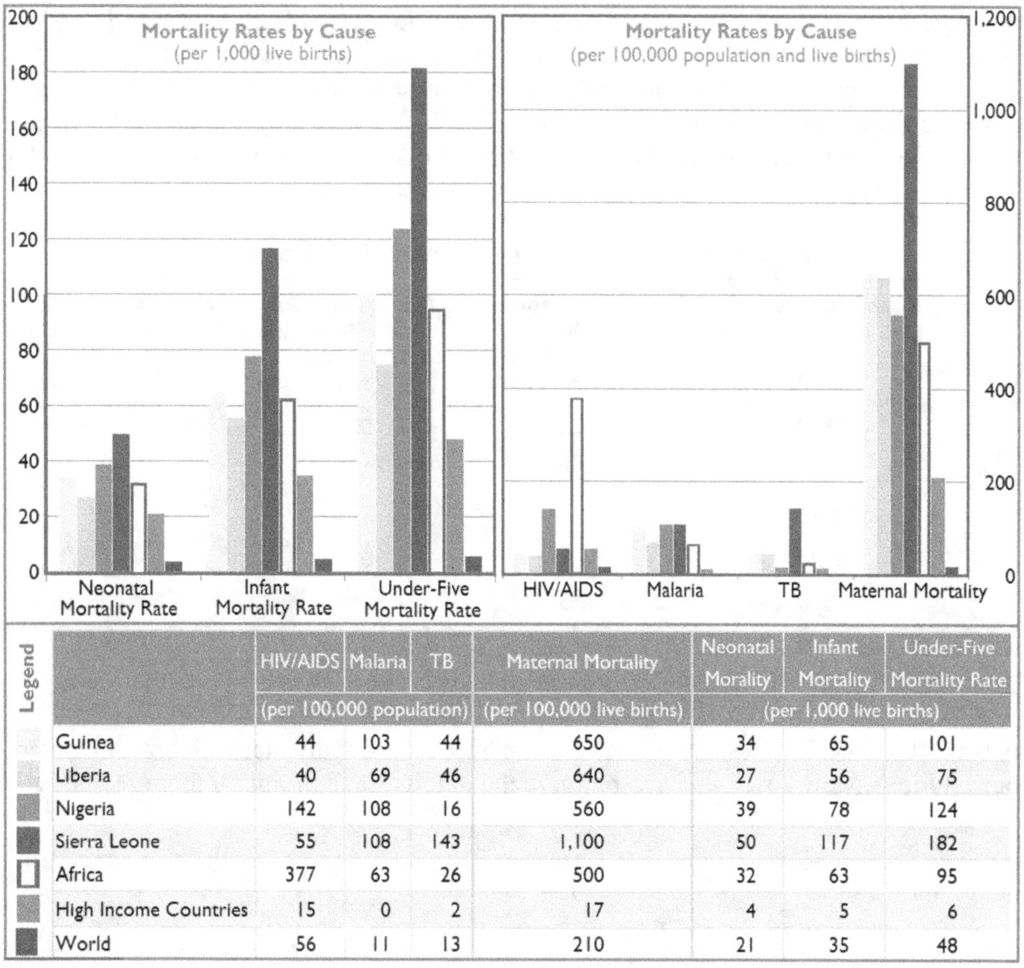

| Legend | | HIV/AIDS | Malaria | TB | Maternal Mortality | Neonatal Morality | Infant Mortality | Under-Five Mortality Rate |
|---|---|---|---|---|---|---|---|---|
| | | (per 100,000 population) | | | (per 100,000 live births) | (per 1,000 live births) | | |
| | Guinea | 44 | 103 | 44 | 650 | 34 | 65 | 101 |
| | Liberia | 40 | 69 | 46 | 640 | 27 | 56 | 75 |
| | Nigeria | 142 | 108 | 16 | 560 | 39 | 78 | 124 |
| | Sierra Leone | 55 | 108 | 143 | 1,100 | 50 | 117 | 182 |
| | Africa | 377 | 63 | 26 | 500 | 32 | 63 | 95 |
| | High Income Countries | 15 | 0 | 2 | 17 | 4 | 5 | 6 |
| | World | 56 | 11 | 13 | 210 | 21 | 35 | 48 |

**Source:** Created by CRS from WHO, *World Health Statistics Report*, 2014.

**Acronym:** Tuberculosis (TB)

**Notes:** *Maternal mortality* refers to the death of a woman while pregnant or within 42 days of a terminated pregnancy from any cause related to or aggravated by the pregnancy or its mismanagement, but not from accidental or incidental causes. *Neonatal mortality* refers to the probability of dying during the first 28 days of life. *Infant Mortality* refers to the probability of dying between birth and one year of life. *Under-Five Mortality* refers to the probability of dying between birth and five years of age. All statistics collected in 2012, except maternal mortality rate, collected in 2013. In 2012 and 2013, the World Bank classified high-income countries as those with gross national incomes of $12,746 or more.

In the four countries, more than 46,000 women died from pregnancy-related complications in 2012, accounting for roughly 26% of all maternal deaths in sub-Saharan Africa.[11] The statistics are similarly startling for childhood deaths in the EVD outbreak countries. In 2012, nearly 1 million children died in the affected countries before reaching their fifth birthday, accounting for roughly 30% of all under-five deaths in sub-Saharan Africa.[12] Most of these deaths could have been prevented with adequate access to vaccines, clean water and sanitation, and nutrition. Experts are concerned that maternal and child mortality rates in these countries will rise as people avoid health clinics and health workers, even when facing life-threatening circumstances like post-labor hemorrhage.

## Financing

Per capita health spending in Guinea, Liberia, and Sierra Leone has been relatively low (**Table 2**), contributing to poor conditions of publicly-funded health facilities. Health workers and other government personnel often experience delays in compensation and benefits. As the Ebola outbreak intensified, some health workers abandoned their posts, citing not only safety concerns (from lack of protective equipment) but also frustration over not receiving salaries. Several local staff at Ebola treatment centers in Liberia had reportedly not been paid for three months.[13]

### Table 2. Selected Health System Financing Statistics, 2011

|  | % of Population Living on < $1 Daily | Health Personnel per 10,000 Pop. | Per Capita Gov. Health Spending | Gov. Health Budget as % of Total Gov. Spending |
|---|---|---|---|---|
| Guinea | 43.3% | not available | $15 | 6.8% |
| Liberia | 83.8% | 2.8 | $27 | 19.1% |
| Sierra Leone | 51.7% | 1.9 | $31 | 12.3% |
| Nigeria | 68.0% | 20.2 | $49 | 6.7% |
| Africa | 51.5% | 14.6 | $76 | 9.7% |
| World | 21.5% | 43.3 | $619 | 15.2% |

**Source:** Created by CRS from WHO, *World Health Statistics Report*, 2014.

**Notes:** Health personnel refers to doctors, nurses, and midwives.

In August 2014, Liberian President Ellen Johnson Sirleaf reportedly met with health workers and apologized for the slow government response to the outbreak and promised more robust actions to

---

[11] UNICEF, *Trends in Maternal Mortality: 1990 to 2013*, 2014.

[12] WHO, *World Health Statistics Report*, 2014.

[13] USAID, *West Africa Ebola Outbreak—Update #2*, August 11, 2014.

end it.[14] The President discussed recent efforts to control the outbreak and address health worker concerns, including completely decontaminating health facilities, transporting food and other social support to people in EVD-quarantine zones, and resolving all outstanding salaries and incentives (such as hazard pay) for healthcare workers—a key complaint among health workers.

**Figure 4. Health Personnel Ratios and EVD Cases Among Health Workers**

(health personnel per 10,000 population)

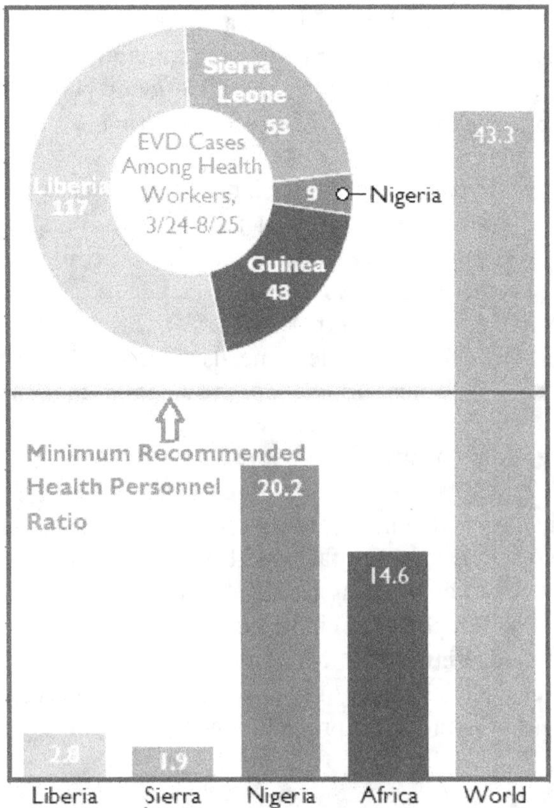

**Source:** Created by CRS from WHO, *World Health Statistics Report*, 2014 and USAID, *West Africa Ebola Outbreak-Update #8*, August 25, 2014.

**Notes:** Health personnel ratio data collected between 2006 and 2013.

All of the outbreak-affected countries lack sufficient financial resources to fund their national plans. Several groups have pledged to provide support to the affected countries, see "International Responses." Sierra Leone estimates it will cost nearly $26 million between July and December 2014 to arrest the spread of EVD in the country.[15] The Government of Sierra Leone has pledged $10 million towards its national response plan and donors have pledged an additional $7.6 million, leaving a funding gap of roughly $8.2 million.[16] The Government of Liberia estimates

---

[14] Government of Liberia, "President Sirleaf Meets with Healthcare Workers; Promised to Settle all Outstanding Incentives Beginning This Week," Press Release, August 10, 2014.

[15] Sierra Leone Ministry of Health, *Sierra Leone Accelerated Ebola Virus Disease Outbreak Response Plan*, 2014.

[16] WHO, "President Koroma visits Ebola epicenters of Kenema and Kailahun and launches revised response plan," (continued...)

that it will need more than $21 million to control the spread of EVD, roughly $6 million of which it has already committed to fund internally.[17] Guinean health officials estimate that the government will need to spend $11 million between July and December 2014 to address the Ebola outbreak.[18] As of July 2014, less than $1 million of those funds had been raised.

## Human Resources

In order to contain Ebola, an array of health and supporting personnel are needed, including healthcare providers who diagnose and treat Ebola cases, epidemiologists and statisticians who study the spread of the disease and inform strategies for containing it, support personnel who safely dispose of deceased EVD patients, and communication experts who relay health information. All of these are in short supply in the affected countries.

Human resource constraints are particularly acute among healthcare providers in the affected countries. Sierra Leone, for example, has fewer than 2 health workers per 10,000 people, far less than the 25 health experts recommend be available per 10,000 people to meet basic health needs (**Figure 4**).[19] Ebola control is labor- and resource-intense, due to requisite containment measures (isolation facilities, protective equipment, expertise in EVD case handling). WHO estimates, for example, that a facility treating 70 Ebola patients needs at least 250 healthcare workers.[20] The affected countries do not have sufficient numbers of providers to meet such demand.

At an August 2014 congressional hearing, one witness testified that prior to the Ebola outbreak, Liberia had fewer than 200 doctors.[21] After the outbreak, he estimated that about 50 doctors remained to provide clinical care, due in part to the evacuation of several expatriate doctors. Existing care providers work longer hours, face additional stress, placing them at greater risk of workplace errors that can lead to contracting Ebola. According to the CDC and WHO, since the Ebola outbreak began, 222 health personnel in the affected countries have contracted Ebola, of whom more than 80 have died (**Figure 4**).[22] More than half of these EVD cases occurred in Liberia, where many nurses have stopped going to work amid concerns about working conditions, including inadequate access to appropriate protective gear, and non-payment of hazard pay.[23]

---

(...continued)

Press Materials, July 30, 2014.

[17] Liberia Ministry of Health, *Liberia Operational Plan for Accelerated Response to Reoccurrence of Ebola Epidemic*, 2014.

[18] Guinea Ministry of Health, *Planned Response to the Ebola Virus Disease Epidemic in Guinea*, 2014.

[19] The Joint Learning, a consortium of one hundred global health leaders, established the ratio after conducting research on maternal and child health. The ratio was cited in WHO, *The World Health Report*, 2006, p. 11.

[20] WHO, "WHO Director-General briefs Geneva UN missions on the Ebola outbreak," Briefing to United Nations Member States, August 12, 2014.

[21] U.S. Congress, House Committee on Foreign Affairs, Subcommittee on Africa, Global Health, Global Human Rights and International Organizations, *Combating the Ebola Threat*, Testimony by Dr. Frank Glover, August 7, 2014.

[22] WHO, "WHO Director-General briefs Geneva UN missions on the Ebola outbreak," Briefing to United Nations Member States, August 12, 2014 and USAID, *West Africa Ebola Outbreak-Update #8*, August 25, 2014.

[23] Richard Preston, "Outbreak," *New Yorker*, August 11, 2014 and BBC, "Sierra Leone chief Ebola doctor infected," July 23, 2014.

# Commodities

The affected countries have limited supplies of protective equipment and not all health and support personnel who interact with the public have access to such equipment. Due to resource constraints, the protective equipment is primarily provided to healthcare workers in Ebola treatment centers, leaving health workers who operate among the general population at risk of contracting and spreading the disease (and other infectious diseases). Health providers also lack sufficient supplies of antibiotics and safe blood to treat Ebola. The price of disinfectants and medicine has reportedly doubled, as people attempt to protect themselves and self-medicate in light of health system deficiencies.[24] Without sufficient tools to prevent and treat Ebola, morale among health workers is reportedly declining.

Observers are also concerned about inadequate diagnostic tools. In each of the three outbreak countries (Guinea, Liberia, and Sierra Leone), only two laboratories are capable of diagnosing Ebola, inhibiting efforts to detect and contain the disease. Without access to rapid diagnostic tests and limited screening procedures (patients self-report symptoms), people who are sick with Ebola may be intermingling with the general population in health facilities. Waiting and treatment areas are filled to capacity with the sick who may be carrying Ebola but cannot be confirmed unless they visit an Ebola treatment center where viral samples are sent for analysis once daily to one of the two laboratories in the affected countries.[25]

# Service Delivery

The Ebola outbreak has further diminished healthcare options in the affected countries. Many health facilities in Liberia and Sierra Leone are closed. As of August 15, in Liberia, all five major hospitals were closed and only three clinics were operating in the capital, Monrovia, and in Sierra Leone, almost no private hospitals were open. Even before the outbreak, access to health clinics was limited. The vast majority of health facilities were concentrated in urban areas, and Ebola outbreak clinics are concentrated in the high prevalence areas (**Figure 2**), leaving large swaths of the population with limited access to healthcare and to Ebola prevention and treatment services.

Due to limited transport options, villagers frequently travel great distances (often on foot) in search of healthcare, prompting most to wait until health complications are severe. Delayed health-seeking practices are reducing survival prospects among those sickened by Ebola and encumbering efforts to detect and contain the virus. The poor conditions of the health facilities also discourage attendance. Power outages and interruptions in potable water delivery are common.[26] In addition, ambulance services are virtually non-existent in rural areas and limited in urban areas. One district in Sierra Leone with a population of 465,000 people reportedly has only four ambulances, which are often overcrowded with ill people, irrespective of Ebola infection status.[27]

---

[24] Newsweek, "Ebola Frontline: Flooding in Sierra Leone Exacerbates Public Health Fears," August 12, 2014.

[25] The Guardian, "State of emergency declared in Liberia and Sierra Leone after Ebola outbreak," July 31, 2014.

[26] Doctors Without Borders, "Flash Quote: WHO Declares Ebola an International Public Health Emergency," Field News, August 8, 2014.

[27] The Star, "In Sierra Leone, an exhausting struggle to contain Ebola," August 18, 2014.

Due to human resource constraints, most countries in sub-Saharan Africa have come to rely on community health workers for healthcare delivery, especially in rural areas. Community health workers are often the first and only providers of healthcare, though they are without formal medical training and are not prepared to distinguish Ebola from other common ailments, including malaria and typhoid fever, which share similar early symptoms. They are particularly vulnerable to contracting and spreading Ebola, due to limited protective equipment. Analysts are concerned that other health efforts not related to Ebola are imperiled.

## Information

Weak government responses coupled with mistrust of government leaders have prompted many to resist Ebola-containment efforts and to ignore Ebola education efforts. Denial is high in Liberia and Sierra Leone about whether Ebola is real, and suspicion about health workers are fueling rumors that they are intentionally infecting people. Other rumors entail cannibalism or the use of Ebola as a ruse to kidnap people and sell their organs. Suspicion about health personnel has been met with violence and has prompted some people to avoid treatment or flee health facilities.[28] On August 16, 2014 in the Liberian capital Monrovia, for example, an armed crowd attacked an Ebola treatment center, emptied it of all care and treatment provisions, and abducted or chased away the patients.[29] Health officials have found the patients who fled, but remain concerned that the incident may have further spread Ebola in the densely populated city.

> *"The International Rescue Committee has seen significant, dramatic declines in service delivery at the health facilities in the past month, because people are rightfully scared to go to the health facility right now. There's going to be a major decline in the number of women who decide to deliver at the health facility, the number of new acceptors of family planning, the number of children who get malaria treatment."*
>
> International Rescue Committee, August 12, 2014.

Due to limited surveillance capacity, there is high uncertainty about the actual number of Ebola cases. One report from the Liberian Health Ministry indicated that the County Surveillance Office in one of the districts with high EVD cases lacks computers for data management.[30] Without sufficient ambulance capacity, dead bodies are reportedly lying in homes and on streets in Liberia with the cause of death undetermined, while backlogs of viral samples are waiting to be tested.[31] On August 23, the Centers for Disease Control and Prevention (CDC) began using a mobile laboratory to conduct rapid onsite testing and ease the backlog.[32]

---

[28] Amanda Taub, "Why Most of the People Ebola Kills May Never Actually Contract It," *Vox*, August 13, 2014.

[29] New York Times, "With Aid Doctors Gone, Ebola Fight Grows Harder," August 16, 2014.

[30] Ibid.

[31] U.S. Congress, House Committee on Foreign Affairs, Subcommittee on Africa, Global Health, Global Human Rights and International Organizations, *Combating the Ebola Threat*, Testimony by Dr. Frank Glover, August 7, 2014 and Doctors Without Borders, "New Strategies, More Resources Needed to Curb Ebola Epidemic," Press Statement, August 15, 2014.

[32] USAID, *West Africa Ebola Outbreak—Update #6*, August 20, 2014.

# Affected Country Responses

Responses to Ebola by the Governments and people of the four affected countries have varied. Nigeria has, to date, prevented the virus from spreading beyond those who had contact with the sole imported case. The other affected countries have been less successful at halting the spread. In Guinea, daily case counts are much lower than in Sierra Leone and Liberia where new cases are rapidly rising (**Figure 5**). Years of turmoil in Liberia and Sierra Leone have eroded trust in those

**Figure 5. 2014 Ebola Cases and Deaths by Country, as Reported on August 22, 2014**

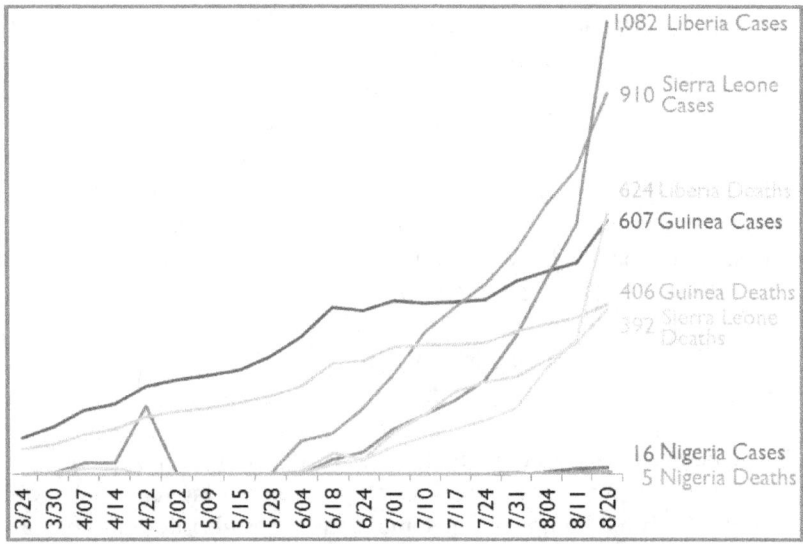

**Source:** Created by CRS from WHO data as reported on the Global Alert and Response website, http://www.who.int/csr/don/archive/disease/ebola/en/.

governments, leading many to resist government containment efforts. Violent responses in Liberia to quarantine zones have increased concerns that the inability to contain the Ebola outbreak could destabilize the affected countries.

Poor civic-government relations have led the Governments of Sierra Leone and Liberia to declare states of emergency, which could enable them to "institute extraordinary measures, including, if need be, the suspensions of certain rights and privileges."[33] Threats of punishment for those harboring Ebola patients or fleeing health facilities[34] and the institution of quarantine zones where police and military forces are barring people from entering or exiting districts with high EVD caseloads (as indicated with polka dots in **Figure 2**) are exacerbating sentiments of mistrust.

The affected countries imposed quarantine zones on districts with high numbers of EVD cases. These zones stretch across 185 square miles and may contain more than 70% of the EVD cases.[35] People in those areas reportedly will be provided with material support and medical attention, and testing and contact tracing efforts in those health areas will purportedly be strengthened. Burial services in those areas will reportedly be done in "accordance with national health regulations,"[36] though in some instances, burial teams have been confronted by members of the community who have refused access to the deceased.

---

[33] Government of Liberia, "President Sirleaf Declares 90-Day State of Emergency, As Governments Steps up the Fight against the Spread of the Ebola Virus Disease," August 6, 2014.

[34] Al Jazeera, "Ebola threatens more West African nations," June 28, 2014.

[35] Joint Declaration of Heads of State and Government of the Mano River Union for the Eradication of Ebola in West Africa, August 1, 2014, http://www.emansion.gov.lr/doc/MRU_EBOLA_jOINT.pdf and Government of Liberia, "MRU Leaders Meet in Conakry, Agree on Measures to Fight the Ebola Viral Disease," August 1, 2014.

[36] Joint Declaration of Heads of State and Government of the Mano River Union for the Eradication of Ebola in West Africa, August 1, 2014.

Sporadic attacks on health workers and clinics, as well as refusal by some to allow health providers access to the sick or deceased is presenting a security challenge for the affected countries. Community resistance to date has mostly been targeted at specific events or facilities, though Liberia is facing increasing incidences of violence as the government tries to use armed forces to impose disease containment measures, which many have defied, and to institute a curfew. On August 20, 2014, the Liberian military reportedly fired live rounds of ammunition to disperse crowds protesting the quarantine measures.[37]

The disruptive effective of quarantine zones have caused some to raise alarm about possible food shortages in the quarantine-affected areas. The World Food Program (WFP) announced in August that it would provide food aid to the roughly 1 million people living in the quarantine zones.[38] Before Ebola hit, hunger was already a problem in the affected countries, particularly in rural areas. Consumption of wild animals is common practice in areas with high food insecurity. Health officials have been expanding efforts to inform the public about the risks associated with eating wild animals, including fruit bats and other animals that might carry EVD.[39] Even if people understand that wild animals may carry EVD, hunger often compels them to continue hunting and eating the animals despite the risks.

Some economists are concerned about the possible economic impact of this outbreak on the affected countries. Government restrictions on the movement of goods and people have reportedly halted commerce in some areas. Cross-border markets have virtually disintegrated, stripping vendors in border territories of their sole source of income. Countless farmers have fled affected zones and delayed sowing crops, raising concerns about food insecurity. Since July, many daily activities have been banned: the Governments of Sierra Leone and Liberia have ordered the closure of schools and markets and put nonessential government staff on mandatory leave.[40] At the same time, some foreign companies are reportedly evacuating workers. A number of mining firms have purportedly withdrawn their foreign staff and shut down non-essential operations. China Union, which began shipping iron ore out of Liberia this year, is reportedly scaling back its activities and considering temporarily halting operations until the outbreak is under control.[41]

# International Responses

On August 8, the World Health Organization Director-General Margaret Chan declared the ongoing Ebola outbreak a "public health emergency of international concern," thereby requiring signatories under the 2005 International Health Regulations (IHR)[42] to report on Ebola cases and other requirements of the IHR. The IHR requires countries to develop national preparedness capacities, including the duty to report internationally significant events, conduct surveillance,

---

[37] USAID, *West Africa Ebola Outbreak—Update #6*, August 20, 2014.

[38] WFP, "WFP Steps Up Assistance to Meet Urgent Food Needs of Families and Communities Affected by Ebola," August 18, 2014.

[39] "Ebola risk unheeded as Guinea's villagers keep on eating fruit bats," *The Guardian*, August 4, 2014.

[40] Justin Moyer, "Liberia closed its borders to contain Ebola. Can that work?" *The Washington Post*, July 31, 2014 and Monica Mark, "State of emergency declared in Liberia and Sierra Leone after Ebola outbreak," *The Guardian*, July 31, 2014.

[41] The Economist, "Panicking only makes it worse," August 16, 2014.

[42] For more information on the IHR see http://www.who.int/ihr/en/.

and exercise public health powers, while balancing human rights and international trade. The IHR can also be used to gauge disparities in disease surveillance capacity and assess efforts by the international community to address them, as signatories of the IHR are required to report annually "on progress achieved in providing support to Member States on compliance with, and implementation of the Regulations on IHR requirements."[43]

The international community, including the United States, is providing support for Ebola responses in the affected countries and WHO is coordinating those efforts. Pledges from multilateral actors include:

- the introduction of a $100 million Ebola response plan by WHO;[44]

- a $210 million pledge from the African Development Bank (ADP);[45]

- the deployment of food and nutritional support by the World Food Program (WFP) to around 1 million people living in the EVD quarantine zones;[46]

- the United Nations Humanitarian Air Service (UNHAS) pledged to provide air transport for aid workers and other stakeholders who are finding it increasingly difficult to travel due to suspended service by commercial airliners.[47]

- a pledge of €11.9 million by the European Union (EU);[48] and

- the provision of $200 million in concessionary loans from the World Bank.[49]

The WHO response plan is intended to fund national Ebola plans. The ADP announced that it will allocate $60 million of its pledge to WHO for its Ebola response. UNHAS is seeking $7.3 million from the international community to fund its transport efforts. The EU funds will be used to expand Doctors Without Borders (known by its French acronym, MSF) operations, provide medical equipment for diagnosing the virus, protective equipment, and support WHO response plan. The World Bank funds will be used to improve disease surveillance and laboratory networks, purchase medical supplies, pay salaries for medical staff, and offer social support for those undergoing financial hardship caused by the epidemic.

Most of the international efforts aimed at supporting national responses to the ongoing outbreak are provided in the form of financial aid, technical assistance, and delivery of commodities, such as protective equipment. The International Rescue Committee (IRC), MSF, and the International Federation of Red Cross and Red Crescent Societies (IFRC) are among the handful of aid groups

---

[43] WHO, *Checklist and Indicators for Monitoring Progress in the Development of IHR Core Capacities in State Parties*, February 2011.

[44] Originally, WHO estimated the regional plan would cost roughly $71 million to implement. See WHO, *Affected Countries Ebola Virus Disease Outbreak Response Plan in West Africa*, 2014. WHO adjusted its estimate to $100 million. See WHO, "WHO Director-General, West African Presidents to Launch Intensified Ebola Outbreak Response Plan," July 31, 2014.

[45] USAID, *West Africa Ebola Outbreak—Update #4*, August 15, 2014.

[46] WFP, "WFP Steps Up Assistance to Meet Urgent Food Needs of Families and Communities Affected by Ebola," August 18, 2014.

[47] USAID, *West Africa Ebola Outbreak—Update #4*, August 15, 2014.

[48] European Commission, *West Africa-Ebola Virus Disease (EVD) Outbreak*, August 11, 2014.

[49] World Bank, "Ebola: World Bank Group Mobilizes Emergency Funding to Fight Epidemic in West Africa," Press Release, August 4, 2014.

providing direct healthcare. Samaritan's Purse closed its health clinics after two of its workers became infected. The affected countries continue to face acute human resource constraints, which the financial aid has not yet sufficiently addressed. Some health experts have criticized the international response, deeming it a "failure"[50] and have implored donors to deploy health providers. According to one MSF doctor, "[d]eclaring Ebola an international public health emergency shows how seriously WHO is taking the current outbreak; but statements won't save lives. It is clear the epidemic will not be contained without a massive deployment on the ground."[51]

## U.S. Responses to Pandemic Threats and Ebola

The United States supports the capacity of foreign nations to prepare and, if necessary, respond to disease outbreaks—including Ebola—primarily through USAID and CDC. The U.S. Departments of Agriculture, Defense and State also contribute to such efforts. These efforts began in earnest after the 2003 SARS outbreak. U.S. responses to the current Ebola outbreak stem from these and other pandemic preparedness efforts. Related activities include providing support for WHO and national Ebola response plans, implementing awareness raising campaigns, bolstering disease surveillance and detection capacity, providing commodities and health supplies, and training police and military forces on the appropriate use of protective equipment. As of August 18, 2014, the United States has deployed 95 personnel to Ebola affected countries (**Table 3**).

**Table 3. U.S. Personnel Deployed to West Africa for Ebola Response**

(as of August 25, 2014)

| Agency or Department | Guinea | Liberia | Sierra Leone | Nigeria |
|---|---|---|---|---|
| CDC | 17 | 21 | 28 | 8 |
| DOD | 0 | 2 | 0 | 0 |
| USAID | 1 | 15 | 3 | 0 |

**Source:** Created by CRS from USAID, *West Africa Ebola Outbreak-Update #8*, August 25, 2014.

## USAID

Recognizing that diseases such as Ebola, H5N1 and H7N9 avian influenzas, and MERS and SARS coronaviruses periodically spill over from animals to cause outbreaks (and sometimes pandemics) in humans, USAID invested a total of $1 billion on pandemic preparedness efforts since 2005. This includes $72.5 million in FY2014 for the Emerging and Pandemic Threats (EPT) program to strengthen the capacity of 18 countries in Africa and Asia to more quickly and effectively detect and respond to infectious disease outbreaks, including Ebola.[52]

The program grew out of USAID's initial response to H5N1 avian influenza in 2005 and is working to identify interventions to reduce the risk of the animal viruses spilling over and spreading in human populations. Congress appropriates funds directly to USAID for EPT. These

---

[50] Science, "WHO declares escalating Ebola outbreak an international emergency," August 8, 2014.

[51] New York Times, "U.N. Agency Calls Ebola Outbreak an International Health Emergency," August 8, 2014.

[52] See the USAID webpage on pandemics at http://www.usaid.gov/what-we-do/global-health/pandemic-influenza-and-other-emerging-threats.

funds have fluctuated between FY2005-FY2014 (**Table 4**). Related activities in 18 countries in East and Central Africa and South and Southeast Asia focus on:

- **viral detection**—identification of viruses in wildlife, livestock, and human populations that may be public health threats;

- **risk determination**—characterization of the potential risk and method of transmission for specific viruses of animal origin;

- **institutionalization of a "one health" approach**—integration of a multisector approach to public health (including animal health and environment);

- **outbreak response capacity**—support for sustainable, country-level response to include preparedness and coordination; and

- **risk reduction**—promotion of actions that minimize or eliminate the potential for the emergence and spread of new viral threats.

### Table 4. USAID Pandemic Preparedness Funding

(current U.S. $ millions and percent)

| | FY05 Actual | FY06 Actual | FY07 Actual | FY08 Actual | FY09 Actual | FY10 Actual | FY11 Actual | FY12 Actual | FY13 Actual | FY14 Estimate | FY15 Request | FY14-FY15 |
|---|---|---|---|---|---|---|---|---|---|---|---|---|
| Avian Flu/ Pandemic Preparedness | 16 | 162 | 161 | 115 | 190 | 106 | 93 | 58 | 55 | 73 | 50 | -31.0% |

**Source:** Created by CRS correspondence with USAID officials, August 6, 2014.

**Note:** Includes supplemental appropriations.

### USAID Ebola Responses[53]

The U.S. Agency for International Development (USAID) has deployed a Disaster Assistance Response Team (DART) to West Africa to coordinate the U.S. Government's response to the Ebola outbreak. The team is overseeing critical areas of the response, such as planning, operations, logistics in coordination with other federal agencies, including the Department of Defense (DOD) and the Department of Health and Human Services (HHS), including CDC.

Between March and August 2014, USAID has provided $14.55 million for combating Ebola in West Africa.[54] Of those funds, $8.95 million from the USAID Global Health Bureau was provided to support the WHO Ebola response plan. This included the provision of 105,000 sets of protective equipment for healthcare staff and outbreak investigators, as well as hygiene kits, soap, bleach, gloves, masks, and other supplies to help prevent the spread of disease.[55] The remaining $5.60 million will be funded through the USAID Office of U.S. Foreign Disaster Assistance

---

[53] Summarized from USAID, "USAID and CDC Announce Additional Assistance for West Africa Ebola Response," press release, August 5, 2014.

[54] U.S. Congress, House Committee on Foreign Affairs, Subcommittee on Africa, Global Health, Global Human Rights and International Organizations, *Combating the Ebola Threat*, Testimony by Ariel Pablos-Méndez, Assistant Administrator for Global Health, USAID, August 7, 2014.

[55] USAID, *USAID Commits More Than $12 Million in Assistance for West African Ebola Response*, press release, August 8, 2014.

(OFDA) to support CDC disease control and detection efforts and to train health ministry staff in the affected countries. OFDA is also supporting the International Federation of Red Cross and Red Crescent Societies (IFRC) to raise public awareness of Ebola's mode of transmission, teach disease prevention practices to communities, train volunteers to detect Ebola symptoms and identify contacts of confirmed or suspected cases for further monitoring, and support safe burial and body management activities. USAID has reprogrammed funds from the Global Heath and International Disaster Assistance accounts to fund these efforts.

# CDC

CDC funds its global pandemic preparedness efforts through a variety of accounts, including the Global Disease Detection (GDD) program, Emerging and Zoonotic Infectious Diseases, Global Health, Immunization and Respiratory Diseases, and Public Health Preparedness and Response. The Centers leverage resources from these and other program accounts to respond to global disease outbreaks—including Ebola. Appropriations for GDD have grown since 2003 (**Table 5**).

### Table 5. CDC Global Disease Detection Funding

(current U.S. $ millions)

|  | FY04 Actual | FY05 Actual | FY06 Actual | FY07 Actual | FY08 Actual | FY09 Actual | FY10 Actual | FY11 Actual | FY12 Actual | FY13 Actual | FY14 Estimate | FY15 Request |
|---|---|---|---|---|---|---|---|---|---|---|---|---|
| GDD | 12 | 21 | 32 | 32 | 31 | 34 | 44 | 42 | 42 | 45 | 45 | 45 |

**Source:** Created by CRS from correspondence with the Office of Management and Budget (OMB), appropriations legislation, and budget justification documents.

CDC has requested additional support ($45 million) in FY2015 to fund activities in support of the Global Health Security Agenda, which will accelerate activities to detect, prevent, and respond to global infectious disease threats like Ebola.[56] CDC directly or indirectly supports pandemic influenza preparedness efforts in more than 50 countries. In some cases, CDC sends experts to work with WHO country offices or foreign health ministries, and at other times, CDC forms cooperative agreements with partners to support country efforts. CDC has also produced public education and prevention messaging posters and factsheets, many of which are picture-based and designed to be accessible to illiterate populations, in the affected countries.

## CDC Ebola Responses[57]

At the end of March 2014, CDC teams traveled to Guinea and Liberia to assist their Health Ministries in characterizing and controlling the outbreak through collection of case reports, interviewing patients and family members, coordinating contact tracing, and consolidating data into centralized databases. Following an initial response which seemed to slow the outbreak for a time, new cases flared up. CDC has since deployed several teams to the West Africa region to help coordinate the response at the national level, assist with database management, and provide health education. CDC is also working with partners to display Ebola-specific travel messages for

---

[56] For more on the Global Health Security Agenda, see http://www.cdc.gov/globalhealth/security/.

[57] This section was summarized from correspondence with CDC. Also see, Meredith Dixon and Ilana Schafer, "Ebola Viral Disease Outbreak – West Africa, 2014," *Morbidity and Mortality Weekly Report* (June 27, 2014), volume 63, issue 25, pp. 548-551; and http://www.cdc.gov/vhf/ebola/outbreaks/guinea/.

electronic monitors and posters at ports of entry to reach travelers from Guinea, Liberia, and Sierra Leone. CDC is not providing direct care of Ebola patients. As of August 5, 2014, CDC has spent approximately $500,000 on staff, supplies and travel for the Ebola response.[58]

## Other Agencies

The State Department is coordinating U.S. responses with affected country host governments and helping to provide public EVD prevention and awareness messaging. It has also monitored regional responses, such as an Economic Community of West African States (ECOWAS) summit and a WHO-led international meeting on Ebola, both held in July.[59] The Department of Defense (DOD), which had health researchers in the region when the outbreak began, is reportedly considering deploying personnel to help address the outbreak and is training armed forces on the appropriate use of protective equipment that it has donated. The goal and makeup of such a deployment has not been determined or publicly announced.[60] DOD also plays a role in supporting drug research and development efforts related to Ebola virus (see Research and Development in the section below).

# Possible Issues for Congress

The current Ebola outbreak has overwhelmed the governments of Guinea, Sierra Leone, and Liberia. Insufficient capacity to detect, treat, and prevent the spread of disease has enabled the virus to spread and has further weakened health systems that were already inundated and in dilapidated conditions. Containing this outbreak may require additional human and material support, as well as technical advice to the affected countries. At an August 2014 congressional hearing, expert witnesses described the dire situation and outlined the scope of required assistance. This section describes issues the 113th Congress might face as it considers these proposals.

## Balancing Funding for Immediate Ebola Responses with Support for Health Systems

The speed at which EVD is spreading across West Africa is attributable, in large part, to weak health systems in those countries. Not only do they face a shortage of trained health workers, but they also lack expertise in disease prevention and containment, including epidemiology, social mobilization, logistics, and case and data management. Expertise in these fields is needed to detect, trace, and contain cases; treat EVD patients; ensure proper use of protective gear; and conduct EVD awareness campaigns. Low salaries in government-funded health facilities contribute to high staff turnover, thereby limiting the availability of health workers and the capacity to ensure consistent and appropriate adherence to disease control protocols.[61]

---

[58] CRS correspondence with CDC, August 5, 2014.

[59] Inter-agency conference call, July 24, 2014.

[60] *Military Times*, "DoD May Send Personnel to Africa to Help Fight Ebola Epidemic," August 1, 2014.

[61] "Ebola cannot be cured but west Africa's epidemic may have been preventable," *The Guardian*, July 8, 2014.

Donors have long grappled with how to address health emergencies in light of dysfunctional health systems. In the early 2000s, donors turned to disease-based funding and channeled health aid through non-governmental groups. Opponents of this approach argued that disease-specific programs exacerbate human resource shortages in the public sector and further weaken health systems when parallel bureaucracies are established and government authorities are bypassed. Supporters assert that disease-based funding strengthens oversight capacity and facilitates the monitoring and evaluation of the investments.

This debate intensified following the introduction of the President's Emergency Plan for AIDS Relief (PEPFAR).[62] In an effort to curb the massive number of deaths that followed the introduction of HIV/AIDS, U.S. agencies provided funding to large non-governmental organizations and local partners who established care and treatment facilities outside of government networks. While the effort helped save millions of lives and averted millions more HIV infections, the United States has become the sole supporter for millions of people worldwide whose lives are at risk should U.S. funding be discontinued. In the second phase of PEPFAR (FY2009-FY2013), increasing portions of PEPFAR resources were used to support health systems in hopes of bolstering country capacity to assume ownership over HIV/AIDS programs. Now in its third phase, debate on the use of PEPFAR funds for building health systems has resumed. A 2013 GAO report noted that roughly 21% of PEPFAR funds were spent on capacity building projects under the "other" budgetary category. At her confirmation hearing, PEPFAR Country Coordinator Deborah Birx asserted that under her leadership, 50% of all PEPFAR resources, including those funded through other accounts, would be spent on care and treatment activities, as mandated. Health system advocates fear that budgetary reforms aimed at adhering to the law may imperil efforts to bolster health systems.

The U.S. Congress faces a similar dilemma with the current Ebola outbreak. The affected countries need focused support to overcome this outbreak. Once this outbreak is arrested, however, the countries will not be in any better position to detect, prevent, or respond to any other disease outbreak unless donors begin the arduous task of supporting the development of strong health systems. Ken Isaacs, Vice President of International Programs and Government Relations at Samaritan's Purse, described this dilemma at an August 2014 congressional hearing on Ebola, "While it should be the goal of the developed world to build capacity, the building of this capacity should not be the focus during times of an emergency crisis of a deadly disease that threatens the international community."[63]

Though PEPFAR and other U.S.-funded health programs have attempted to respond to calls for greater investment in health systems, no appropriations specifically targeting such efforts are provided. Language in appropriations and accompanying conference reports direct the majority of health aid to particular diseases, leaving minimal resources for broader activities to strengthen health systems. As Congress considers responses to the current Ebola outbreak, as well as FY2015 appropriations, it may debate the appropriate mix of disease-specific and health system strengthening support. The inability of the affected countries to contain the Ebola outbreak may be a factor in congressional consideration of the $45 million sought by the CDC to fund the

---

[62] For more on PEPFAR, see CRS Report IF00042, *The President's Emergency Plan for AIDS Relief (PEPFAR): Summary of Recent Developments* (In Focus) and CRS Report R42776, *The President's Emergency Plan for AIDS Relief (PEPFAR): Funding Issues After a Decade of Implementation, FY2004-FY2013*, by Tiaji Salaam-Blyther

[63] U.S. Congress, House Committee on Foreign Affairs, Subcommittee on Africa, Global Health, Global Human Rights and International Organizations, *Combating the Ebola Threat*, Testimony by Ken Isaacs, Vice President of International Programs and Government Relations, Samaritan's Purse, August 7, 2014

newly announced Global Health Security agenda. Congress may also consider calls from some health experts who call for the establishment of a "Health Systems Fund," to be administered by WHO.[64]

## Evaluating U.S. Responses

A variety of U.S. agencies are responding to the ongoing Ebola outbreak. The Department of State is leading diplomatic engagements; USAID is coordinating U.S. responses, including the provision of financial and material support; CDC is heading public health and medical response activities; and DOD is handling support for foreign armed forces. With the exception of USAID, the budgetary structure of each of these agencies enables them to respond to this unanticipated event by drawing from other internal accounts. The Department of State's efforts to coordinate bilateral diplomatic engagements are likely conducted through existing channels (e.g., embassy contacts) and, as such, would not require additional, dedicated funding. Outbreak responses by the CDC can be financed through USAID disaster assistance accounts, as well as several CDC accounts that are used for domestic and international health efforts and for which there is not explicit congressional direction on their use. Since DOD responses typically focus on force protection, engagement with foreign countries can be funded through an array of activities that support that mandate.

The appropriate use and level of support to provide for foreign assistance is often strongly debated in Congress and as a result, Congress has established numerous directives over the years on how foreign aid funds are to be used. As the lead U.S. development agency, USAID often receives specific direction from Congress on how the bulk of its funds will be used through annual appropriations, leaving the agency with limited ability to address unanticipated events, like the current Ebola outbreak, without drawing from ongoing health efforts. According to USAID, it is currently reprogramming funds planned for preventing future outbreaks, as well as addressing ongoing outbreaks (including responses to H7N9 avian influenza in China and MERS-CoV in the Middle East), to address the current Ebola outbreak.[65]

Supporters of the current appropriation structure see it as a tool for overseeing health programs and ensuring that congressional priorities are met. Opponents argue that congressional directives encumber the agility that is needed in the field and create artificial segmentation of health and development issues, thereby limiting the impact and sustainability of such efforts.

By their nature, disease outbreaks are often unpredictable, though with appropriate disease surveillance, detection, and response mechanisms, their impact can be minimized. At present, USAID pandemic preparedness efforts are focused on East and Central Africa as well as South and Southeast Asia, where previous Ebola and influenza outbreaks have occurred. Now that Ebola has emerged in West Africa, it is highly probable that another Ebola outbreak may occur in the region, a scenario countries in the region are ill-prepared to handle. The FY2015 budget request ($50 million) for pandemic preparedness is roughly 30% less than the FY2014 funding level ($73 million). Even if Congress funds USAID pandemic preparedness programs at the

---

[64] Lawrence Gostin, "West Africa's Ebola Epidemic is Out of Control, But Never Had to Happen," Briefing Paper Number 9, August 20, 2014. For more on the possible structure and functions of the Global Health Fund, see Lawrence Gostin and Eric Friedman, "Towards a Framework Convention on Global Health: A Transformative Agenda for Global Health Justice," *Yale Journal of Health Policy, Law, and Ethics*, (2013), volume 13, issue 1.

[65] CRS correspondence with USAID, August 5, 2014.

---

FY2014 funding level, one USAID official contends that it will not be enough to meet current demands.[66]

## Addressing the Long-Term and Broader Effects of the Outbreak

The Ebola outbreak may cause several long-term and broader effects in the region. Under the best of circumstances, experts predict that it will take at least six months to get the outbreak under control. MSF has reported that some affected villages in Sierra Leone have lost the majority of adult community members, leaving vulnerable populations—such as children and the elderly— without resources to cultivate agricultural land and procure food.[67] Observers are also concerned about a growing number of children who are being orphaned from Ebola. This group is particularly vulnerable to marginalization due to overwhelming fear of the virus. Countries in West and Central Africa already had large orphan populations due to a variety of causes including armed conflict and HIV/AIDS. In 2012, some 28 million children were orphaned in the region, of whom more than 4 million lost one or more parent to AIDS.[68]

Ebola is also hindering the capacity of these governments to address other health issues, such as obstetrical complications. Experts are concerned that child and maternal mortality rates, already high in the region, may further rise due to diminishing numbers of health personnel (caused both by Ebola deaths and abandonment of posts), diversion of limited resources to Ebola treatment centers, and public avoidance of health centers.

The full health effects of the Ebola outbreak may not be known until it is contained. An accounting of broader health and development needs will likely ensue and may rekindle debate over how U.S. global health assistance funds are apportioned. Since PEPFAR was launched, global health advocates have debated the appropriate share of global health resources HIV/AIDS programs should consume. Though U.S. global health programs are aimed at a range of global health problems, appropriations for combating global HIV/AIDS comprise the bulk of U.S. global health funding.[69] Congress is likely to face arguments from advocates from a variety of actors attempting to garner support for a bevy of health and development issues that will have likely worsened in the wake of Ebola, including maternal and child mortality, child vulnerability and orphanhood, poverty, food scarcity, and water-borne infections.

## Considering Research and Development Needs

Since 1976, several Ebola outbreaks have erupted in sub-Saharan Africa, yet therapeutic options remain undeveloped. There is no cure, specific treatment regimen, or vaccine to prevent Ebola, nor or is there any post-exposure prophylaxis for health workers who face regular exposure. Treatment of EVD symptoms increases the probability of survival. The appropriate use of experimental drugs that have not been tested for human safety and effectiveness has become a matter of debate, particularly around the issue of equity.

---

[66] Ibid.

[67] USAID, *West Africa Ebola Outbreak—Update # 5*, August 18, 2014.

[68] UNICEF, *Towards an AIDS-Free Generation Children and AIDS: Sixth Stocktaking Report*, 2013.

[69] For more on U.S. global health funding, see CRS Report R43115, *U.S. Global Health Assistance: FY2001-FY2015 Funding and Issues for Congress.*

In early August 2014, two Americans healthcare workers who became infected with Ebola while working in Liberia were given an experimental antibody treatment, called ZMapp™, that was not approved in the United Sates or any other country, and had not been tested in humans.[70] A global health lawyer described the ensuing debate. "Should [U.S.] workers receive a drug in extremely scarce supply when Africans are affected in far greater numbers? Balanced against this sense of injustice is the ethical concern of administering an experimental drug to African patients that has not undergone any safety testing in humans."[71] In addition, if the experimental drugs are ineffectual or cause serious side effects, then their use may further exacerbate mistrust in healthcare workers and modern medical treatments. WHO held a special meeting in August on the topic and announced that under "the particular circumstances of th[e] outbreak, and provided certain conditions are met ... it is ethical to offer unproven interventions with as yet unknown efficacy and adverse effects, as potential treatment or prevention."[72]

Since the announcement, the United States has provided three courses of the ZMapp™ to Liberia and the three Liberian health workers who received the drug are reportedly recovering.[73] The DOD Defense Threat Reduction Agency (DTRA) is providing additional funding to the manufacturer to extend research on the drug.[74] In addition to ZMapp™, other drugs and vaccines are under development and several countries have reported having unapproved medicines and vaccines that they believe may be effective in treating and preventing Ebola.[75] The National Institute of Allergy and Infectious Disease (NIAID) at the National Institutes of Health (NIH), for example, is funding the development of an Ebola vaccine.[76] Trials are expected to start in September 2014.

While some observers are optimistic about the potentially life-saving effects of ZMapp™, others including the manufacturer, caution that the efficacy of the drug has not yet been determined and that all available supply on the drug has been exhausted.[77] Very few courses of the drug were developed because it is still in the experimental stage and the manufacturer does not have the capacity to develop large quantities of the treatment.[78] One health expert estimates that it might take at least two years before a safe and approved drug or vaccine is available for clinicians.[79]

---

[70] Andrew Pollack, "Ebola Therapy from an Obscure Biotech Firm Is Hurried Along," *The New York Times,* August 6, 2014. See also CDC, "Questions and Answers on Experimental Treatments and Vaccines for Ebola," August 8, 2014, http://www.cdc.gov/vhf/ebola/outbreaks/guinea/qa-experimental-treatments.html.

[71] Lawrence Gostin et al., "The Ebola Epidemic: A Global Health Emergency," *JAMA,* (August 11, 2014).

[72] WHO, "Ethical considerations for use of unregistered interventions for Ebola viral disease (EVD)," WHO statement, August 12, 2014.

[73] Wall Street Journal, "Second American Ebola Virus Patient Gaining Strength," August 19, 2014.

[74] Global Biodefense, "MAPP Biopharmaceutical Awarded Funding for Ebola Drug," July 30, 2014, http://globalbiodefense.com/2014/07/30/mapp-biopharmaceutical-awarded-funding-ebola-drug/ and FedBizOpps.Gov, "MB-2003: An Ebola Virus Countermeasure," Solicitation Number HDTRA1—13-C-0018-P00003, July 22, 2014.

[75] "Japan prepared to supply unapproved medicine to Ebola-hit W. Africa," *Mainichi,* August 25, 2014; "Canada to donate experimental Ebola vaccine," *CTV News,* August 12, 2014.

[76] NIAID webpage on *Ebola/Marbug Research* at http://www niaid nih.gov/topics/ebolaMarburg/research/Pages/default.aspx.

[77] Mapp Biopharmaceutical, "ZMapp™ Frequently Asked Questions," and information on Mapp Biopharmaceutical homepage, August 12, 2014, accessed on August 20, 2014.

[78] CDC, "Questions and Answers on Experimental Treatments and Vaccines for Ebola," webpage on the 2014 West Africa Outbreak, accessed on August 20, 2014.

[79] Doctors Without Borders, "Ebola Specialist: Experimental Drugs Inspire Hope, but Crisis Continues in West Africa," Voices from the Field, August 8, 2014.

---

CDC underscores that the most effective way to stop the ongoing Ebola outbreak is to follow the same protocols that halted past Ebola outbreaks: "meticulous work in finding Ebola cases, isolating and caring for those patients, and tracing contacts to stop the chains of transmission."[80]

# Conclusion

The rapid spread and high death toll of the current Ebola outbreak is causing panic within the affected countries, as well as many other countries worldwide. In the affected countries, leaders are instituting quarantine measures, prohibiting free movement of people in entire districts. CDC asserts that the implementation of quarantines is an ineffective approach to limiting the spread of EVD and that the action could limit access health care and case tracing, further inhibiting EVD response efforts.[81] Several people in the quarantine zones have met these actions with violence and have deepened their resentment and mistrust of government leaders. Violent outbreaks within the countries, particularly in Liberia, are troubling to some observers who fear the inability of the governments to contain the virus and their efforts to control population flows may lead to broader unrest and deepen hunger and poverty, particularly in quarantine zones.

Although WHO maintains that there is little risk of contracting Ebola on an airplane, a growing number of countries are barring people from Guinea, Liberia, and Sierra Leone from entering their territories, and an increasing cadre of commercial airlines is cancelling flights originating from the affected countries. Several international actors have expressed concern about Senegal's decision to close its borders, airports, and seaports to arrivals from the EVD-affected countries, as the country serves as a key operational hub for humanitarian shipments. At the same time, suspended air travel is hampering the ability to move health workers and material assistance within and among the affected countries, further inhibiting Ebola response efforts.

Some economists and health experts are concerned about the broader impact that the outbreak and global responses to it are having on the countries. The World Bank has already reduced projected economic growth estimates for Guinea. People in the affected countries, already faced with limited healthcare options before the Ebola outbreak, have almost no access to health services that are not related to Ebola, as many hospitals in the affected countries have closed since health workers began contracting Ebola. At the same time, many of the expatriate health workers who supplemented the paltry health workforce in those countries have evacuated.

Concerns about protecting health workers from Ebola, as well as attacks by fearful citizenry, have possibly discouraged countries from sending health experts to care for Ebola patients. The United States and other donor countries have sent teams of experts and other forms of assistance to the affected countries, though the aid has been provided primarily in the form of material aid and technical assistance.

The inability of the affected countries to contain the ongoing Ebola outbreak is a testament of the poor health infrastructures in those areas. As Congress considers responses to this outbreak, debate may center not only on the levels and types of assistance to fund, but also on how to balance funding for immediate Ebola responses against the need for broader health system

---

[80] CDC, "Questions and Answers on Experimental Treatments and Vaccines for Ebola," webpage on the 2014 West Africa Outbreak, accessed on August 20, 2014.

[81] USAID, *West Africa Outbreak –Outbreak #8*, August 25, 2014.

strengthening efforts. Congress may also consider the long-term assistance these countries may need as their economies and infrastructures are further decimated by the ongoing outbreak.

# Author Contact Information

Tiaji Salaam-Blyther
Specialist in Global Health
tsalaam@crs.loc.gov, 7-7677